By Laura Williams
Translated by Lee Ji-su

© 2022 Williams Books
1 rue de l'église, 91430 Igny
Dépôt légal : Décembre 2022
ISBN 978-2-494614-45-1
Imprimé à la demande par Amazon
Loi n° 49-956 du 16 juillet 1949 sur les publications destinées à la jeunesse

영양
[yeong-yang] – antelope

박쥐
[bagjwi] – bat

곰
[gom] – bear

빈대
[bindae] – bedbug

꿀벌

[kkulbeol] – bee

물소

[mulso] – buffalo

나비
[nabi] – butterfly

낙타
[nagta] – camel

고양이

[goyang-i] – cat

카멜레온

[kamelle-on] – chameleon

병아리
[byeong-ali] – chick

닭
[dalg] – chicken

바퀴벌레

[bakwibeolle] – cockroach

젖소

[jeojso] – cow

귀뚜라미
[gwittulami] – cricket

악어
[ag-eo] – crocodile

개
[gae] – dog

당나귀
[dangnagwi] – donkey

오리
[oli] – duck

지렁이
[jileong-i] – earthworm

코끼리

[kokkili] – elephant

물고기

[mulgogi] – fish

파리
[pali] – fly

여우
[yeou] – fox

개구리
[gaeguli] – frog

가젤 영양
[gajel yeong-yang] – gazelle

기린
[gilin] – giraffe

염소
[yeomso] – goat

거위
[geowi] – goose

하마
[hama] – hipopotamus

말
[mal] – horse

하이에나
[haiena] – hyena

사자

[saja] – lion

도마뱀

[domabaem] – lizard

두더지
[dudeoji] – mole

몽구스
[mong-guseu] – mongoose

원숭이

[wonsung-i] – monkey

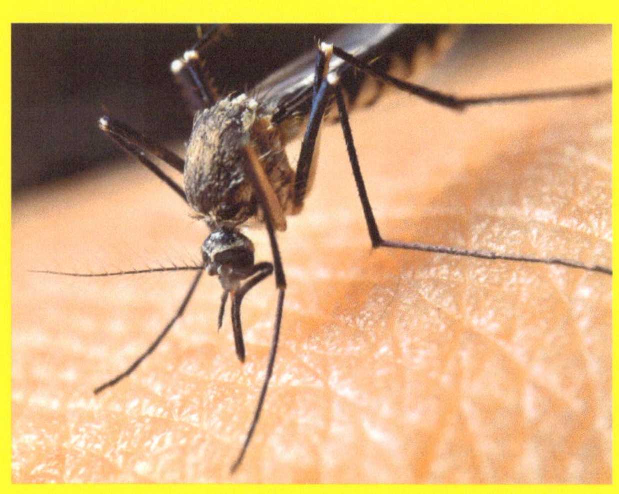

모기

[mogi] – mosquito

쥐
[jwi] – mouse

앵무새
[aengmusae] – parrot

돼지
[dwaeji] – pig

비둘기
[bidulgi] – pigeon

토끼
[tokki] – rabbit

수탉
[sutalg] – rooster

양
[yang] – sheep

달팽이
[dalpaeng-i] – snail

뱀
[baem] – snake

거미
[geomi] – spider

말벌

[malbeol] – wasp

얼룩말

[eollugmal] – zebra

Thank you

Thank you for purchasing "Korean-English Words for Toddlers"! Your support means a lot to me, and I hope you and your child enjoy these books.

If you have a moment, I would greatly appreciate it if you could leave a review on Amazon. Your feedback will help me improve future editions of the series and create more resources for bilingual children.

Thank you again for your support. You can access the reviews on Amazon by scanning the QR code below or by visiting the link below:

https://www.amazon.com/review/create-review?&asin=2494614457

Thank you for helping me continue my work as a language teacher and translator. Your support is greatly appreciated!

In the same collection